Gus Finds His Smile

A Children's Guide to Building a Healthy Perspective

Written by Cathy Studer

Illustrated by Sona and Jacob

Printed in the USA

Published by Author Academy Elite

PO Box 43, Powell, Ohio 43065

www.authoracademyelite.com

Library of Congress Control Number: 2022913979

Paperback ISBN: 979-8-88583-101-7

Hardcover ISBN: 979-8-88583-102-4

Ebook ISBN: 979-8-88583-103-1

Illustrations and Cover Design by Sona and Jacob

This Book Belongs to

____

Dedications and Acknowledgements

To my angel hero in heaven—Mom, thank you for being an example of what a hero should be, your incredible demonstration of resilience, and your love. You are forever in my heart and thoughts.

To my father in heaven—Dad, I will be forever grateful for your amazing example of what a good perspective should be. You always wanted to see the good in people and situations. I appreciated that and emulated that in my life because of you. You are forever in my heart and thoughts.

To my sister in heaven—Candy, I know you are with me as I write this set of books. Thank you for keeping mom and dad company with your beautiful smile and love.

To my husband and support here on Earth—Mike, thank you for your love and for accepting and embracing my next passion project.

To my amazing kids—Dustin and Carissa, I am proud of you for walking your journeys with perseverance, excellence, and belief in yourselves. I love you dearly!

Thank you to the following people:

Illustrators - Sona and Jacob

Editors - Sandra Duclos, Deanna Stevens, and Charlene Lindsey

Beta Readers - Sonya Harle, Lisa Ruman, Lori Poland, Parker Huston, Angela Tjugum, and Julie Blackford

Special shout out to Mrs. Miller's second grade class at East Linden Elementary and Mrs. Hedrick's first grade class at Arrowhead Elementary for being beta-classrooms!

Thank you to the CASA volunteer in Cuyahoga County who encouraged me to write this set of books.

Praise for *Gus Finds His Smile*

"A heartwarming story to help children learn how to cultivate a balanced mindset. It's a helpful resource for anyone who works with children, and it includes practical tips for helping the children in your life apply these valuable attributes."

-Parker L. Huston, PhD
Pediatric Psychologist

"As an elementary educator for more than thirty years, I am saddened by the number of students who struggle with overwhelming feelings of sadness, frustration, and worry. This book is a must-read to teach children how to deal with the pressures of childhood while focusing on their positive experiences. You will fall in love with furry little characters, Gus and Pasha, as Pasha helps Gus find his smile and a positive perspective in life. Parents and teachers alike will find this book a very helpful teaching tool. It provides a springboard for powerful discussions on positive mental health with elementary-aged children."

-Sonya Harle, MEd
Elementary Educator

"Gus Finds His Smile *is a beautiful story about hope and connection. Cathy's ability to put words to such common confusion for children is truly remarkable. She highlights the beauty of friendship, possibility, and the value of optimism, even when life is challenging. So well done to help create strong, healthy mindsets."*

-Lori Poland, MA, LPC
Former CEO , The National Foundation to End Child Abuse and Neglect

"Cathy Studer's heart-warming children's story addresses the importance of open communication. It doubles as a read-aloud for both SEL (social-emotional learning) goals and many of the reading standards for young learners. This is an excellent tool for teachers to help their students grow mentally and emotionally."

-Lisa Ruman
ESL Teacher, Columbus City Schools

SWISH, SWISH, PLOP...SWISH, SWISH, PLOP!

The noise abruptly woke Gus the gorilla from his nap. He stood and watched quietly from behind the tree as Pasha the panda played by the lake. She skipped stones across the water and smiled as the sun shone on her little black nose and fuzzy black ears.

Why is she so happy? Gus wondered as he watched her play.

He walked closer to see why she kept smiling.

"Hi Gus! Come skip stones with me!" Pasha said excitedly.

"Okay, but I don't know how to skip stones," Gus said shyly.

"I'll show you. Watch me," Pasha said. "Move your wrist like this and then toss the rock." Her stone skipped across the water three times.

Gus picked up a stone, moved his wrist twice, as Pasha had done, then threw his stone.

PLOP!

It fell right into the water and dropped to the bottom of the lake. His face showed his disappointment. "I can't do anything right."

"Gus, that was your first try. Watch me, then try it again," Pasha said with encouragement.

Gus picked up another stone and tried to skip it across the lake. The stone fell into the water with one big loud plop and sank to the bottom again.

"See! Nothing ever goes right for me." Gus yelled and stomped his foot on the ground.

"Come here, Gus. Let's sit and talk." The two furry friends sat down next to the lake.
"Gus, we need to find your smile. Why are you so hard on yourself today?"
Gus had his head down and spoke quietly, "I don't know. I guess I just feel sad, frustrated, and worried."

"It's good to talk about how we feel, especially when we're sad." Pasha put her paw on Gus's shoulder. "Can you tell me what is making you feel this way?" Pasha asked.

"Hmm, no one has ever asked me that." Gus lifted his head as he thought about her question.
"I guess I worry that the other animals don't like me. I can't do things well and it makes me sad and frustrated. And when my mom and dad argue, I feel uncomfortable."

Pasha listened and thought for a moment. "That's a lot of worries, Gus. I bet that does make you feel sad and frustrated. Has anyone said they didn't like you?"

"Well, Greg was really mean to me yesterday," Gus said sadly as a tear rolled down his furry face.

"I'm sorry Gus, I bet that did hurt." Pasha nodded and put her paw on top of Gus's hand.

"I try to ignore those who are mean to me. We have many other animals to play with in the forest. Choose friends who you have fun with and the ones who like you just the way you are. Find friends who enjoy spending time with you, like me! Gus, you'll never be alone with me as your friend."

Gus grinned shyly. "Awe, thank you, Pasha."
"When I worry about stuff I can't control, it makes me feel sad and anxious too," shared Pasha while she held Gus's hands.
"I have learned that most of the things I worry about never happen. That means I was sad and worried for no reason."

"But how are you so happy?
Do you never have a bad day?"
Gus crosses his arms.

"Do things always go right
for you?" Gus asked.

"I'm not always happy.
Yesterday, I had a terrible day. I spilled my breakfast, got in trouble at school for talking too much, and my brother was mean to me. Before dinner, I sat down and cried. Crying is okay. Tears help let my sadness out, and I always feel better afterward."

Gus tilted his head and listened closely to Pasha.

"Let me share what else helps me feel happy. I look for something good in my day." Pasha held her paw out as she spoke.

"Even on my yucky days, I can find something that is good. When I focus on the good things, it makes me feel happier. Yesterday after I cried, I started to focus on how much I enjoyed helping my mom bake a sweet treat after supper. Then I started to feel my smile come back. Sometimes, even simply smiling makes me feel happy."

Pasha smiled as she thought about it.

"I don't know
if I can do that,
Pasha." Gus's shiny,
black furry head
was down again.

"Let's try, Gus. Yesterday, you felt sad because Greg was mean to you. Can you remember something good about yesterday?" Pasha hoped her words would encourage Gus, who looked like he was thinking hard.
"Well ... I had my favorite lunch yesterday, and I also got a frozen banana as a special treat before bedtime. Hmm ... oh! Then my mom read me a book before I fell asleep."

"Now you got it, Gus! Wow, that's three good things that happened in one day! It's okay to think about the bad things, but when we put *more* focus on the good things, it helps us feel a lot less sad and worried."

Pasha put her arms around Gus and squeezed him in a hug.

Then Pasha jumped up. "Come on, let's try skipping stones again. Watch my wrist closely." Pasha moved her wrist a few times and then threw a round gray stone. It skipped twice across the water.

"Okay, I'll try," Gus said as he stood up. He picked up a stone and practiced with his wrist a couple times before he tossed it across the water. Much to his surprise, the gray, oval stone skipped four times across the lake.

"Look at you, Gus! That was fantastic!" Pasha cheered.

"I did it!" Gus jumped and shouted as he threw both arms up in the air. "That felt great! Thank you for showing me how to skip rocks, Pasha."

The two friends stood together at the edge of the water as they threw their stones. Some stones skipped, some stones did not, yet they laughed and enjoyed each other's company the entire time.

"I have to go now, Pasha," Gus said. "I'm supposed to be home before dark." As Gus turned to leave, he looked back at Pasha.
"I *will* work on finding good things in my life, even on my bad, yucky days. Oh, I just thought of something that is very good about today."
"What is that?" Pasha asked.

"Having you for a friend," he said.

Gus ran back to Pasha and gave her a big gorilla hug. Although he was not great at skipping stones yet, he skipped himself home as the sun went down, happy he found his smile.

Resources for Parents Grandparents Foster Parents Teachers Counselors

How to Help Children Build a Healthier Perspective

Summary of Key Points

- Building a healthy perspective requires us to focus on more than the negative. When we worry frequently or only think about the unpleasant things, we can feel anxious.
  - We can reduce anxiety when we acknowledge the negative, feel the emotion, and then let it go!
- As we focus more often on positive things, our brains shift, the anxiety reduces, and we are able to create more joy.
- If your child worries more than typical or continues to focus on the negative in their life, guide them to notice their thoughts and then shift their worry to finding the good.

The key to helping our children is to guide them toward positive thoughts to build stronger mental and emotional health.

Activities & Conversation Starters

- After reading about Gus finding his smile, ask your child to share one or two good things about their day. These don't have to be "big" things. We can find good in the little things when we look for it.
- At mealtimes, make it a habit to invite everyone around the table to share one good thing about their day. (This is a great activity to practice in the car, too.)
  - When we think positive thoughts, they become good words.
  - Then those good words become good actions, which then become valuable habits.
  - When we establish valuable habits, we rework the brain to build stronger mental and emotional health.
- If your child has the toy characters from the book, initiate play time with Pasha and Gus and encourage the child to use the toys to act out what they learned from the story.
  - Children learn so much through play as it provides a safe way to release their emotions. Practicing what they have learned helps instill a valuable habit of seeing the good in life and releasing worries or sadness.

Want to learn more about why our perspective matters for our mental health?

If you would like more tips supporting children to a healthier mindset, check out the extra free guide to this book.

Learn More

Kintsugi

Kintsugi is the Japanese art of repairing broken pottery with lacquered silver or gold. It highlights the cracks instead of hiding them, reflecting the belief that we can make a broken article stronger and more beautifully whole. This art form teaches us to embrace our imperfections and to realize that we can become stronger after our mistakes or hardships.

Each book in this set of six is a fun tool for parents, teachers, and counselors to help guide children to build stronger mental and emotional health. These books teach the attributes printed on the above Kintsugi piece that, once adopted, act as the lacquer of silver or gold in strengthening us. The attributes work the brain to develop a healthy mindset. Kintsugi is the metaphor I used in my book *Broken to Beautifully Whole*.

All children will encounter challenges, pain, or trauma in their life. Let's equip them to handle such hardship by strengthening their mental and emotional health. Doing so is easier with young children because their brains are so malleable. All children deserve empowerment to fulfill their best potential.

Let's do this, together!

About the Author

As a young girl and into adulthood, perspective was one of the six key attributes Cathy Studer developed to help overcome difficult circumstances. After healing from childhood trauma, she found her purpose in teaching these attributes to children and adults to help build a foundation for stronger mental and emotional health.

She is the award-winning author of *Broken to Beautifully Whole*, and a mental health advocate, child abuse prevention advocate, and speaker. Cathy also facilitates the *Stewards of Children* program to empower organizations and parents to prevent child sexual abuse.

She is passionate about guiding those who have experienced brokenness or mental health issues to reclaim wholeness, uncover purpose, and discover the power to reach their full potential.

Cathy lives in Ohio with her husband and their yellow lab, Levi. She loves spending time with her two adult children and two grand dogs.

The Adventures of Gus and Pasha

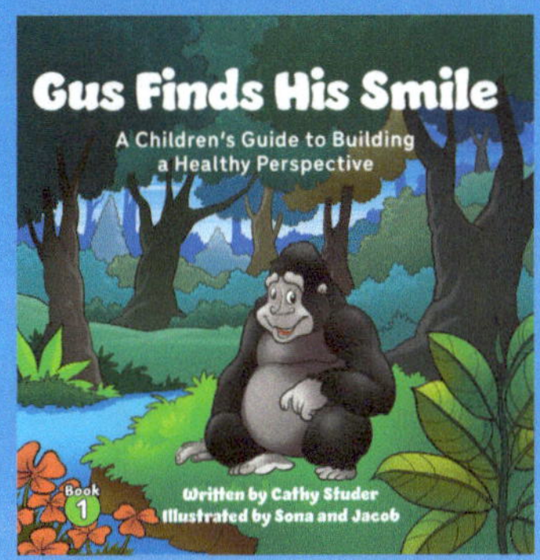

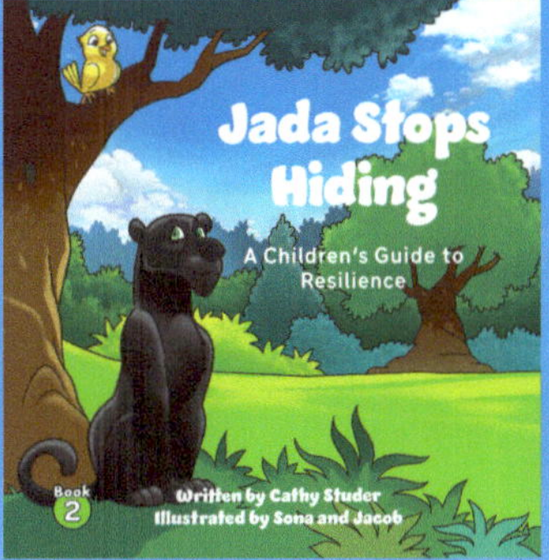

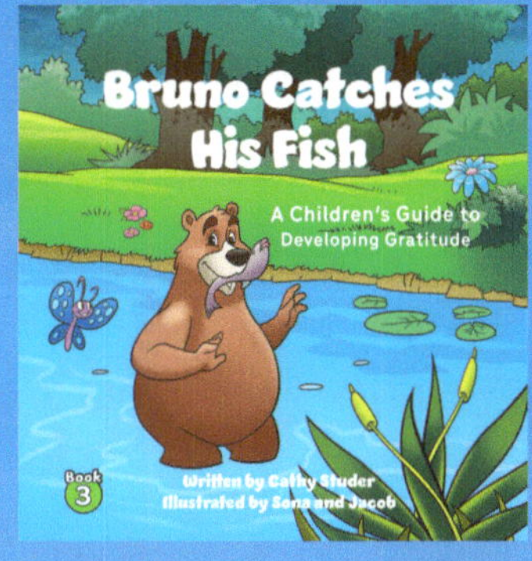

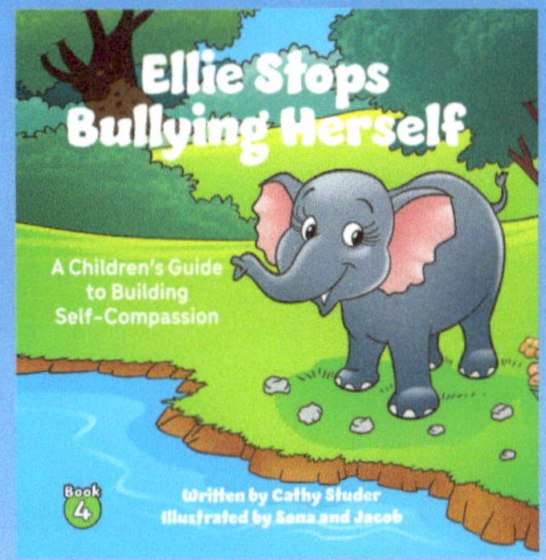

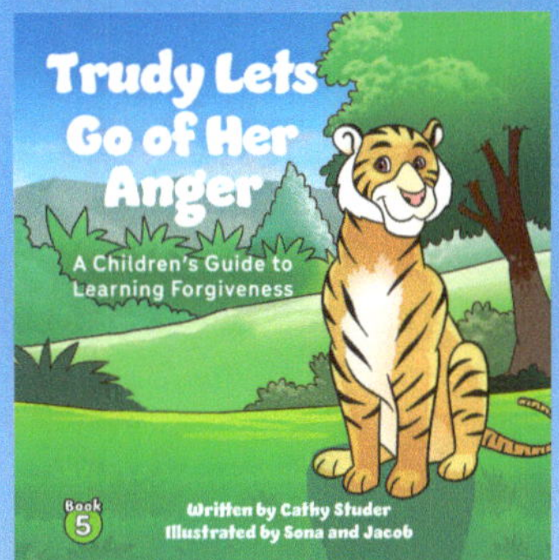

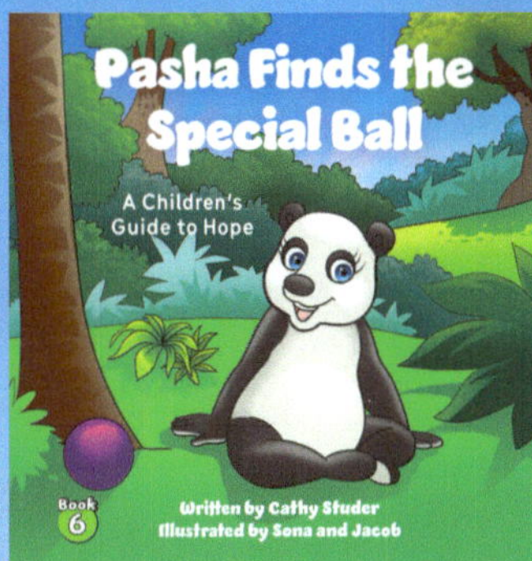

There is tremendous value in reading the series in order as the books build upon one another.

Check out all six books in the series.

www.ingramcontent.com/pod-product-compliance
Lightning Source LLC
Chambersburg PA
CBHW042111110726
48006CB00002B/598

* 9 7 9 8 8 8 5 8 3 1 0 1 7 *